Shorelines

Also by Mishka Lavigne

from Éditions l'Interligne
Cinéma (2016)
Havre (2018)
Copeaux (2020)
Murs (2023)

from Playwrights Canada Press
Haven (translated by Neil Blackadder, 2023)

Shorelines
Mishka Lavigne

Playwrights Canada Press
Toronto

Shorelines © Copyright 2023 by Mishka Lavigne
First edition: September 2023
Printed and bound in Canada by Imprimerie Gauvin, Gatineau

Jacket art by Mélanie Simoneau
Author photo © Marianne Duval

Playwrights Canada Press
202-269 Richmond St. w., Toronto, ON M5V 1X1
416.703.0013 | info@playwrightscanada.com | www.playwrightscanada.com

For professional or amateur production rights, please contact:
Catherine Mensour, Mensour Agency
kate@mensour.ca | 613.241.1677

LIBRARY AND ARCHIVES CANADA CATALOGUING IN PUBLICATION
Title: Shorelines / Mishka Lavigne.
Names: Lavigne, Mishka, 1984- author.
Description: A play.
Identifiers: Canadiana (print) 2023046999X | Canadiana (ebook) 20230470025
    | ISBN 9780369104618 (softcover) | ISBN 9780369104625 (PDF)
    | ISBN 9780369104632 (EPUB)
Classification: LCC PS8623.A835355 S56 2023 | DDC C812/.6—dc23

Playwrights Canada Press operates on land which is the current and ancestral
home of the Anishinaabe Nations (Ojibwe / Chippewa, Odawa, Potawatomi,
Algonquin, Saulteaux, Nipissing, and Mississauga), the Wendat, and the members of the Haudenosaunee Confederacy (Mohawk, Oneida, Onondaga, Cayuga,
Seneca, and Tuscarora), as well as Metis and Inuit peoples. It always was and always
will be Indigenous land.

We acknowledge the financial support of the Canada Council for the Arts, the
Ontario Arts Council (OAC), Ontario Creates, and the Government of Canada for
our publishing activities.

Shorelines was first produced by TACTICS as part of their MainStage Series at LabO, Ottawa, from May 2 to 13, 2023, with the following cast and creative team:

Featuring: Jacqui Du Toit, Letréal Farquharson, Vanessa Onukagha, and Cara Pantalone

Director: Nicholas Leno
Dramaturg: Emily Pearlman
Set Design: Brian Smith
Costume Design: Hannah Ferguson
Sound Design: Ali Berkok
Lighting Design: Tristan-Olivier Breiding
Stage Manager: Jane Osborn
Production Manager: Shanice Pereira

Characters

Alix: seventeen years old, seven minutes older than Evan
Evan: seventeen years old, seven minutes younger than Alix
Portia: older
Gran: unable to hold on to reality / The Voice of Gran: a shattered
memory

Setting

The humidity and heat are suffocating.
There is a swimming pool.
It's empty, cracked, and filled with mud, leaves, and twigs.
It's been empty for years. Decades.
Despite everything, the pool is a sanctuary.
Everything is in various stages of collapse.
Including them.

Prologue

Darkness.
Sirens.
Everything feels half real.

Lights on ALIX *and* EVAN, *soaked to the bone, holding hands.*
A flash, then darkness again.

Lights flash on PORTIA.
Water drips from her hair, her clothing, pools at her feet on the
floor.
Darkness.

Slowly, lights come up on GRAN, *standing, staring straight*
ahead.

THE VOICE OF GRAN *(at first a whisper, over or under)*
Hierochloe odorata.
Thuja occidentalis.
Artemisia tridentata.
Cypripedium candidum.
Pedicularis furbishiae.
Panthera pardus orientalis.
Panthera tigris tigris, so long ago.
Balaenoptera physalus.
Gorilla beringei, habitat loss.

Monodon monoceros, as the Arctic melted.
Vulpes lagopus.
Ursus arctos horribilis.
Ursus maritimus, of course.
Apis mellifera mellifera, in the wild, gone.
Zingiberales musaceae.
Coffea canephora.
Theobroma cacao.
Carcharodon carcharias, from the deep.
Bison bison bison.
Danaus plexippus, lost in migration.
Eretmochelys imbricata.
Eubalaena glacialis.
cities
entire cities
islands
glaciers
forests . . .

Lights at their brightest.

GRAN
I'm swimming in a pool.

Darkness.

One

EVAN is alone in the empty pool, sitting on the steps or on the bottom. He is sweaty and dirty. ALIX drops into the pool.

EVAN
Hey.

ALIX *(handing EVAN a label-less can)*
Look what I found.

EVAN
What is it?

ALIX
No label.

EVAN
Add it to the pile.

ALIX goes to a waterproof box in a corner, opens it to put the can in.

ALIX
Is that all we have left?

EVAN
I used some of the canned fruits to trade for soap.

ALIX
What time did you leave this morning?

EVAN
I don't know. Early. You were still sleeping by Gran's bed. I wanted to have time to get to the old docks by the shoreline.

    Beat.

ALIX
Evan . . .

EVAN
I know.

    Beat. EVAN stares ahead.

ALIX
Gran woke me up at 2 this morning, speaking in Latin.

EVAN
Again?

ALIX
She wanted to bake bread in the middle of the night, but when she opened the metal box with the flour, it was flecked with mould and she cried.

EVAN
Is the water back at Gran's? I didn't bother to check.

ALIX
You know it isn't. We'll have to get more Salt-No rations at the base.

EVAN
I'm so tired of Salt-No water.

ALIX
I've heard the desalinating machine at the base is barely working, it keeps breaking down. They've ordered new parts for it but it's been weeks and nothing. That's what this soldier told me.

EVAN
Which soldier? The one I saw you talking to last week?

ALIX
His name is Jackson . . . He's been sneaking me extra rations of Salt-No.

EVAN
In exchange for . . .

ALIX
For nothing.

EVAN
Sure.

ALIX
I traded some of the extra rations around town. I got you this.

> She hands EVAN a small figurine of an elephant.

For your collection.

EVAN
It's not a collection.

ALIX
Then what do you call the bag of animal figurines you keep in the filtration trap?

EVAN
Not a collection. I just find them . . . fun, okay?

ALIX
It's okay, you're allowed to have a collection.

EVAN
It's not a collection!

ALIX
Fine! I got you this non-collectible animal friend. Better?

> *Beat.* EVAN *takes the elephant figurine, pockets it.*

EVAN
Thank you.

> *Beat.*

I'll head down to the shoreline again. See if I can find a few more things to trade. Someone told me about an old storage facility where a few of the units are still locked. Are you in?

ALIX
I should get home. See how Gran is doing.

EVAN
If I were you, I'd take a nap. You look like shit.

ALIX
Shut up.

Beat.

EVAN
The other day, I looked out the window in the middle of the night and Gran was standing out in the street. I think she's been sneaking out by the side door with the busted lock. She can't keep wandering outside in the dark—it's not safe.

ALIX
I'll figure something out. I'll ask around, see if someone can help me repair the lock.

EVAN
I can help. With Gran, I mean.

ALIX
It's fine. I don't need help.

Beat.

I'll see you at Gran's.

EVAN
See you later.

ALIX
Be careful.

EVAN *(rolling his eyes)*
Yes, Mother.

> *ALIX leaves. EVAN takes the elephant figurine, goes to the filtration trap, and takes out a bag. He delicately places the animal in the bag and hides the bag again.*

Two

ALIX, alone.

ALIX
Jackson's room on the army base isn't really a room
it's a closet
no windows
sliding metal door
but it has A/C
most of the time.
I love it.
I've been hanging around every Tuesday and Wednesday for
weeks now.

No one sees me go in.

He has a bed, a box with clothes, a few books, and an old picture
pinned to the wall.
A woman.
Pretty.

Who is she?

"She's my mom," he says.
"She died when I was two. Malaria."

My mom died of malaria too.
When I was five.
And my dad is—

He says he's sorry.
We don't speak for a while.

We sit on his bed.

He says he has a gift for me.
He takes it out from under his bed.
It's water, real water, not Salt-No, not that machine-desalinated crap.
Real spring water, especially in glass bottles, is really expensive.
He says his dad sent it to him for his birthday.
It tastes like . . . something I had a long time ago.

His eyes are begging me to stay.
He takes his finger and collects a drop of water from the corner of
my mouth
then places his finger on my bottom lip.
My lips part and I lick the water on his finger with the tip of my
tongue.
He exhales gently.
His finger
out of my mouth
traces the line of my jaw
down my neck to my collarbone
it lingers.

"How old are you again?" he asks.

I lie.

Nineteen, I say. Nineteen soon.

Two years is soon.
Soon-ish.

It doesn't hurt.
I thought it would.
Maybe I'm just different.

He says my skin tastes like salt.
I say I'm sorry.
He kisses my eyelids, my throat, the soft space just above my hip bone.

"Don't say you're sorry. I love it."

Three

*EVAN, in the pool. He lines up dozens of animal figurines and
toys on the edge of the pool.*

EVAN
It's really dangerous. Everyone knows it is.
But it's not like there's anything else to do.

Salvage.

People have been doing it for years:
roaming around the shorelines,
salvaging and trading whatever is left behind.
And some, like my dad, got more creative with it.

There are sunken cities everywhere now.
Houses under water, half-submerged buildings.

My dad has an old sailboat and diving gear.
Before he got the diving gear,
he would just have to stay on the upper floors:
the ones that sat above the waterline.
The upper floors are the ones that got picked out the quickest.
Combed thoroughly
licked clean
like bones.

He can be out on his boat for days sometimes.
It takes longer to reach the taller towers on the other side of the
bay now.
That means the water is still rising.

Sometimes, when he finds something really good
he sails to the old docks
the ones that are lower on the shoreline
the ones that are submerged for most of the year,
you can still see some of their metal posts stick out of the water.
Birds perch on them.

When you come in at the old docks,
you don't have to declare your salvage to the authorities.

Every morning, very early,
when the fog still rolls in from the water
and makes it easier to hide a boat from the patrols,
I wait for him at the old docks.

I've been waiting
every day
for the past sixteen days.
He's never been gone that long.

The first time he was out on his boat overnight, Alix and I were twelve.
He came back the following afternoon
covered in mud, tired and drained.
And in his coat pocket, he had two little figurines of cats.
One for Alix: a grey cat curled into a ball around three grey and white
kittens.
And one for me: a black cat with a red bow around its neck.
He found them in an apartment he salvaged, he said.

Alix broke hers, or lost hers, a while back, but I kept mine.
Funny how you find figurines like these everywhere
even when you're not looking for them.
Clay figurines, glass figurines, plastic toys.
Animals.
It's not a collection.
It's just—
I see them and I can't just leave them there.
I just can't.

   Beat.

I keep having these nightmares where my father vanishes
disappears in the water-filled ghost rooms of some office building
trapped by a destroyed ceiling or under a piece of furniture
his oxygen tank slowly emptying.

When I get these dreams,
I wake up drenched in sweat.
I look at Alix sleeping in the room next door, or in Gran's room.
She misses him too. I know she does.
She acts all tough but she can't hide anything from me.

I wake up from nightmares and run to the old docks.

I wait.

My dad is not dead.
He's coming back.
I know he is.

Four

ALIX. EVAN.
THE VOICE OF GRAN / GRAN.
PORTIA.

ALIX
Before we found this pool, we used to hang out in an old house by the
shoreline.
We spent all of our time there, even if it was dangerous.
Everything along the shoreline is dangerous anyway.

EVAN
We hung out in what used to be a bedroom.
There was still a bed frame, old and rusted.

ALIX
Inside the house
you could hear water dripping
all the time
just drip, drip, drip.

PORTIA
Years had passed.
Years.

THE VOICE OF GRAN
Twins are the most common form of multiple human births. They account for around 4% of all births.

PORTIA
I tell myself
it's a town like any other
it's a shoreline town like any other.
But I know this, here, is different.

ALIX
One day, we decided to see where the dripping sound was coming from.
We climbed to the attic and found leaks in the roof.
Water just seeping in between the rafters—
drip, drip, drip—
all over the attic floor.
There was a part of the floor where water was pooling.
We started playing a game.
A game to see which one of us would get the closest to the puddle of water.

PORTIA
I didn't tell anyone.
No one on my staff
no one at the office
not even my drivers or military escorts.
No one can know.
I walk around the base
greet soldiers
thank them for their service.

THE VOICE OF GRAN

A multiple pregnancy can be monozygotic, where one zygote splits
into two embryos, resulting in identical twins, or dizygotic, where each
egg is fertilized from a separate sperm cell, resulting in fraternal twins.
Male and female twins cannot be identical.

EVAN & ALIX

Stupid.
Dangerous.
We knew it.
We were just
bored.

GRAN

I had a twin once. Identical. Laura. I remember when she died.

PORTIA

When I arrived at the military base yesterday
the commander showed me a map of the current shoreline
and right there
at the bottom of the map
I saw it:
the Mercury Tower Apartments
a tiny little street block
lost in the dark grey mass
of the condemned part of town.

ALIX

We stood around on the spongy wood floor
and inched closer and closer to the edge of the puddle.
We laughed.

We pushed each other.
Closer and closer.
Until the floor gave way under me
and I fell
all the way down
to the floor of the master bedroom
my stomach inches away from the metal bed frame.

GRAN
I know it's not scientific. It has never been scientifically proven. But
I know it, deep down. I remember it. Laura died and I suddenly felt
. . . hollow. And cold.

ALIX
The wind was knocked out of me.
The room was spinning.
I could almost feel the metal spikes of the bedframe embedded in my
spine.

EVAN
Alix fell and I stopped breathing.
Pain searing through my rib cage, spots of darkness blurring my vision.
I wasn't hurt. She was.
And I felt it.

PORTIA
The commander escorts me to an empty hangar where a podium is
set up.
A soldier sits behind a camera
another holds a microphone.
"Are you ready, ma'am?"
asks the commander.
I stand behind the podium

smooth my hair down
pick a piece of lint from my jacket.
I bring up the communiqué on the podium screen.
I smile.
Ready.

GRAN
Laura died. Cancer. Her body was rotting from the inside out. I
was sitting by her bed at the hospital. The little A/C unit in her
window was humming and softly dripping little droplets of water
into a saucer—drip, drip, drip—but the air in the room was still too
warm. It was early March. It hadn't snowed at all that winter. Was it
the first winter it hadn't snowed? Or the second? I don't remember
anymore . . .

EVAN
We never went back.
A few weeks later we found this pool.
Can't fall through a pool.

GRAN
My eyes were closed. I was tired, tired from the hospital, the heat,
dead tired. I was pregnant but I didn't know it yet. Laura died. It just
happened and I felt it. A sudden wave of cold. And emptiness. I didn't
even need to open my eyes: I knew.

PORTIA
The camera's little light blinks once, twice, three times
then becomes solid red.
The soldier behind the camera signals with her fingers.
And I freeze.
I was about to speak
and I just can't.

GRAN
Laura was thirty-nine when she died. I was thirty-nine when I became a Half. A Half with a zygote growing inside me. A single fertilized zygote. Your father.

PORTIA
"Ma'am?" the commander asks.
I just need a bit of water, I answer.
He hands me a small can of Salt-No.
I drink it and it leaves a strange film on my teeth.
I forgot Salt-No did this.

EVAN
There's a logo painted on the bottom of the pool.
An "M" or a "W" in a circle.
Alix and I found an old rickety metal porch swing, dragged it here, and set it up in the pool.
We have our bins with our things to trade, tarps for when it rains.
We even brought tomato seeds from one of the neighbours.
We planted them in an old rain barrel, but they're not growing.
The seeds are probably just rotted by the salt in the dirt we used.

GRAN
There are no specific genetic factors that contribute to twin births. We used to think there were. We used to say "twins run in the family." But they don't. It's random.

EVAN
That old house ended up being swallowed by the water.

PORTIA
I drink another sip of Salt-No.
Let's go again, I say.

The camera light blinks once, twice, three times.
Go.

GRAN
Seventeen years ago, when you were born, and then Evan, seven minutes after you, I remember thinking about Laura. Your father asked me if they could name you Laura. I said no. No sense in naming a brandnew baby girl with a dead woman's name. No sense.

ALIX
Gran?

EVAN
Are you okay, Gran?

GRAN
Apollo and Artemis. Fraternal twins. The sun. The moon.

EVAN *(to ALIX)*
Maybe she's just tired. It's getting late.

ALIX
What are you saying, Gran?

GRAN
Nothing, Laura, nothing. Go back to sleep. You need your rest.

Five

PORTIA

The 2067-9K Act proposes the restructuration of the lower shoreline to eliminate superfluous energy being diverted to empty cities.

As a government, we are forced to face the fact that the water containment systems are failing, that we do not have enough energy to keep the levees from breaking under the force of the water. Populations will have to be displaced, brought up from the shorelines. The government will help with the resettlement of these populations. Jobs will be found, housing for families, schools for children. We are doing everything we can to minimize the impact of this resettlement.

No one left behind. This is a promise this government is willing to make.

The shoreline is ever-changing. A strong and conscientious leadership will help you face the challenges of tomorrow. We are living in dangerous times. Let us help you.

Our plan is simple: a total and complete evacuation of this city.

In thirty-six hours, a convoy of buses will gather at the military base. These buses will take you and your family towards a better life out west. Permits and passes will be issued for your travel needs. With these documents, travel bans will be lifted as long as you are travelling on the government-sanctioned vehicles.

Once you have arrived at your destination, you will be housed in temporary facilities, pending processing. School-age children will be administered tests in order to ease their transition into public education once the processing period is over. Adults will be administered questionnaires to better help with job placement. Everyone will receive necessary health exams, vaccinations, and health care. Once processing is done, citizens will be re-homed into various western cities and districts.

To board buses, we ask citizens being evacuated to gather the following documents for all adults and minor children: identity cards, birth records, union or marriage records, and any land deeds, leases, or mortgage documents, including those for property or properties considered under water.

Do not worry. Everything will be taken care of. We have done this before and with great success. Small cities and settlements all along the shoreline are being evacuated at this very moment. Today, it's your turn. This government has your best interest at heart. This government cares.

In thirty-six hours, you will be heading west.
Brighter days are ahead.

This is a promise.

Six

EVAN is sitting alone in the pool. ALIX drops in.

ALIX
Did you see the broadcast? The evacuation orders?

EVAN
Yeah . . . I saw it.

ALIX *(taking out a sheet of paper from her pocket)*
They nailed it to the door at Gran's too.

> *EVAN takes the paper from ALIX, reads it, crumples it, and put it in his pocket.*

Don't we want to be evacuated?

EVAN
What will it change? You heard the rumours of people who were evacuated . . . I don't want to spend ten years in a refugee camp just to be sent to a city that's going to get evacuated again when the water reaches it. We're better off here than in some camp out west.

ALIX
We're not better off if they turn off the power for good, if the army leaves, if everyone's gone. We can't stay here.

EVAN
Mom and Dad are here.

ALIX
Mom and Dad are dead.

Beat.

Sorry. Dad is—

EVAN
Can you even pretend you have a little bit of hope?

ALIX
Sixteen days, Evan. I just—

EVAN
Okay.

Beat.

ALIX
Gran doesn't get what's happening with the evacuation. I explained it to her a bunch of times. I even brought her to the base to see the broadcast earlier this afternoon. It's playing on a loop in the community area.

EVAN
Any excuse to go to the base, right?

ALIX
It's not like that. I wanted Gran to see the video. I thought it would help her understand.

EVAN
And you just happen to run into your little soldier lover and sneak off to a broom closet?

ALIX
Stop it.

EVAN
You may think he's different but he's the same as these other soldiers. Do you think they care about any of us at all? Do you think they care about this city, about the people in it? They're just rich kids, using their two years of army reserve to get better jobs, to get university placements once they get out. They're here to do a job and they don't need to care about us.

ALIX
Jackson is not like that. And it's none of your business, Evan. I can do whatever I want.

EVAN
Fine!

ALIX
Fine!

 Beat.

EVAN
Where's Gran now?

ALIX
I took her home, then I came here to find you.

EVAN
Why?

ALIX
Something strange happened.

EVAN
What?

ALIX
When we were in the community centre at the base watching the broadcast, Gran had one of her lucid moments. She saw the woman on the screen and lost it. She kept calling her Catherine. But that's not her name. The government representative.

EVAN
No. It's Portia something.

ALIX
Yeah. Portia Lowell-James.

EVAN
Why is that weird? Gran is confused. What else is new?

ALIX
You didn't see her face. She was convinced that woman was called Catherine. She made a scene at the base. A soldier even told me I had to take her home because she was upsetting other people.

EVAN
Is she okay now?

ALIX
When we got home, she looked perfectly normal. Not good or lucid or anything. Just her regular self. It was so weird.

EVAN
If you say so.

Beat.

ALIX
We need to leave this place, Evan. You know we do.

EVAN
What if he comes back and we're not here anymore?

ALIX
He'll know where we are. The evacuation orders are posted all over town. We'll be with Gran on the government buses. There's no way he won't find us. The army will probably stay behind for a few days to handle stragglers.

Beat.

EVAN
He's coming back.

ALIX
He's coming back.

Beat.

I'll go pack Gran's things.

ALIX leaves. EVAN stays alone. He takes the evacuation orders out of his pocket, reads them again, smooths out the paper, folds it meticulously, and puts it in his pocket.

Seven

GRAN's voice can be over or under.

EVAN
Gran used to be a journalist.
Our dad showed us some of her articles.
Gran used to print them out:
articles like hers had a way of vanishing from the web back then.

THE VOICE OF GRAN
Permafrost is rock or cryotic soil at or below the freezing point of 0°
Celsius for more than two years.

EVAN
Gran was a scientific journalist.
She worked for the biggest news agencies
she gave conferences
university lectures
she was always travelling.

THE VOICE OF GRAN
Most permafrost occurs in high latitudes, around the Arctic and
Antarctic circles, but alpine permafrost can also occur at lower lati-
tudes but higher altitudes.

EVAN
Dad got to go with her everywhere.
Him and Gran would travel for months at a time.
She would home-school Dad on the road.

"The world is changing. Faster than any scientific model could have
predicted."

I read this in one of her articles.

THE VOICE OF GRAN
In 2012, Russian scientists revived a flowering plant, *Silene stenophylla*,
from a thirty-thousand-year-old specimen of seed and tissues.

EVAN
Gran was at the 2015 Paris Climate Change Conference.
She was working for Associated Press at the time.
It was before Dad was born.
I read and reread her articles on the Paris Conference.
I try to hear her voice as I'm reading them.
But I can only seem to hear her today.
Her rambling thoughts
her Latin words
all the nonsense sentences she speaks in the shadows of the mouldy
kitchen.

THE VOICE OF GRAN
In 2016, large quantities of the anthrax virus, liberated by the thawing
permafrost in Siberia, contaminated herds of reindeer and members of
nomadic Indigenous populations dependent on reindeer-herding for
survival.

EVAN
Dad is good with her.
Alix is really good with her.
Whenever she looks at me
I just feel useless.

THE VOICE OF GRAN
The Arctic permafrost is the largest deposit of mercury in the world.
Rapid thawing of the Arctic sheet ice and permafrost is releasing large
quantities of mercury into the air and into the oceans.

EVAN
I can't seem to recognize
the person I saw in the videos.
The person I read in the articles.
The person Dad told me about.
Can't seem to reconcile
Gran then
and Gran now.
She's fading away.

GRAN
. . . *Eubalaena glacialis*, silent songs, depths of silence, *Balaenoptera borealis*, I'm so thirsty, all the time . . . it's the salt . . . *Balaenoptera musculus*, it's because of the salt . . . *Balaenoptera physalus*, *Gadus morhua*, *Carcharodon carcharias*, *Monodon monoceros*, the deep, where the light doesn't reach, *Tursiops truncatus*, *Thunnus alalunga*, *Salmo salar* . . .

Eight

PORTIA
I head out through the main gate and no one stops me.
I walk away from the base, downhill towards the shoreline.

I walk.

Everything is drained of colour
like looking at a photograph of a photograph.
I walk for a long time until I arrive right in front of a barricade:
the condemned neighbourhoods nearer to the shoreline.

There's a gap in the fence and I crawl through.
On the other side, it's like a different world.
Even the small traces of order that still exist in this town are absent.
The streets are cracked
large pieces of roadway simply missing
gaping holes of crumbling cement and metal rebar.
Houses are in shambles
windows broken
roof shingles missing
cracked foundations, vines growing out of the crevices
pieces of furniture here and there.
I press on.
A few streets over, you can clearly see the outlines of floods etched
onto the sides of the houses that are still standing.

I walk among the wreckage.
The sky is grey and night is starting to fall.
I know I should head back to the base
head back to the relative safety of the other side of the barricade,
but I walk until I see it:
the Mercury Tower Apartments.

I walk to the other side of the tower.
I count out the floors
        five
        six
        seven
On the seventh floor
I count the windows
        ten
        eleven
        twelve
I can almost see the blue and grey curtains billow out
but, of course, there's nothing there except a hole where a window used
to be.

My bedroom.
The bedroom I shared with my cousin Simon.

I walk behind the tower.
The door is hanging precariously off its hinges.
I slip in through the opening
right onto the landing of the back staircase.
The cement steps are cracked, held up by a rusted metal frame.
I look up, and above, there's only total darkness.
I take a flashlight from my pocket and aim it upwards:
only a few more steps, and then nothing.

The staircase is completely missing.
Someone must have drilled through it to steal the metal rebar.

No way up.

On the landing,
a lone cockroach scuttles from one pile of wet trash to another.
I exit the building.
The sky is dark, and in the distance, thunder rumbles.
Rain starts to fall, muffled by the spongy ground.
One of those evening storms with hail and wind.
We used to get them all the time when I was younger.
I could see them blow in from the water from my bedroom window on
the seventh floor.

On this side,
in the shadow of the Mercury Tower,
there was a pool.
It was this place's only luxury.

A pool.

I walk towards the pool
ignoring the rain that's getting stronger.

I just need to see it again.

The sky is getting even darker now
there's a slight haze to the air
and a metallic smell wafts from the ground.
Lightning rips the sky open, the thunder is deafening.
All around me rain falls

heavy curtains of water.
I can't see anything.
Another bolt of lightning
even closer this time.
I need to take cover.
I look behind me.
I can't even see the tower in the rain.
I double back in its general direction.
I walk as fast as I can
bracing against the wind
my body catching in brambles and branches.
It has to be close to here.
And suddenly,
my feet are carried away in a mudslide.
I can't feel solid ground under me
my hands helplessly try to hold on to something
      roots
      vines
      branches
      breaking.

And I fall.

I land hard on my leg
pain shoots all the way up to my hip
      crack
      bone
my knee gives out
right arm bracing for impact
my head slams forward
      darkness.

Nine

ALIX. EVAN. Not together.

ALIX
I'm swimming in a pool.
The water is cool and clean and clear.
The sun shines through the water and makes everything sparkle.
Evan is there. My dad too.
Even Gran is there.
She has on this beautiful white summer hat with a wide brim and a
green ribbon.
It's a party and there's food and glasses filled with little round ice cubes.
Everyone is happy.

EVAN
I'm on my dad's boat.
The sail billows in the wind, the sky is blue, and the water shines like
diamonds.
I lie on my belly on the deck, watch the water rush past the sides of
the boat.
Behind me, my dad and Alix and Gran laugh and talk.

ALIX
I get out of the pool and wrap myself in a fluffy blue towel.
Gran hands me a glass of water filled with ice
and I drink it, and it's cold and nice and it doesn't taste like salt at all.

People laugh and talk and there is music playing.
I sit on the concrete edge of the pool and put my feet in.

EVAN
Seabirds are circling above.
Gran knows all of their names, calls them out.
I turn over on my back and stare up at the cloudless sky.
The sun is so bright.
I close my eyes and my eyelids shine red.

Suddenly, silence.

I open my eyes, sit up.
I'm alone.

Dad? Alix?
Dad!?

ALIX
Suddenly I'm alone.
Clouds gather.
The air gets cold.
The water becomes dark and murky and I can't see the bottom of the
pool anymore.
A rancid smell wafts in.
The water is blanketed in dark sludge.
I take my feet out of the water and they're covered in angry red blisters.

EVAN
I look around,
water everywhere,
no land in sight.

The sun beats down on me.
I'm thirsty. Really thirsty.

Dad?

ALIX
In the pool
A dark shape floats towards me:
a body,
face down in the water,
limbs swollen and bruised,
hair hanging limp like weeds.
The body rolls over in the water and slowly its face emerges from
the muck.

EVAN
I grab on to the rope railing, dip my hand in the water, bring it up,
drink.
Salt.
I dip my hand in the water again.
Again. Again. Again.
The salt water makes my stomach hurt.
The sun burns my skin, my lips, my eyes.

I'm completely alone.

The wind dies down and the sail hangs limply on its hooks.
The sun sets and darkness comes.

I'm alone.

ALIX
The body rolls over
and I'm staring at myself
my body
drowned
broken
skin sloughing off
my face
lips black
eyes bulging.

I drop the glass of ice water I was still holding in my hand
it falls onto the concrete
and shatters
glass shards and ice shards
everywhere.

In the water
the body—
my body—
opens its eyes.

Ten

GRAN

I open my eyes.

On the cot by my bed, Alix is still sleeping.

It always happens in the morning. Moments of feeling like myself. Sometimes an hour or so, when I wake up, and I know exactly where I am, who I am, who's sleeping by my bed.

It used to be like this every day. Things would start to fade in the evening, then in the afternoon. But I always had mornings. Then most mornings. And now, I know it's not every day. Not even every week. Looking out the window, I know time has passed without me. Time passes without me inside. And I'm terrified.

Alix looks like her mother. Evan looks more like my son Karl did at that age, but Alix is all Audrey. Maybe a faint little echo of my sister Laura in the voice.

I sit in bed. Alix stirs, rolls over, and falls back asleep.

I reach my hand out to her
maybe we could talk for a bit
like we did
before.

But I don't touch her.
I don't want to wake her up.
She needs her rest.

At the foot of the bed, there's a bag, half filled with clothing. This
girl doesn't know how to pack a suitcase. I used to be so good at it.
Travelling all the time. I look at the bag. Why is it there? Where are we
going?

I get out of bed and walk to the kitchen. On the table, there's a flyer.
Evacuation orders. I read the flyer but the letters are starting to dance
on the paper. That name at the bottom of the page . . . Portia. Her
name is Portia . . . no, that's not it. I know it isn't. And somewhere in
the back of my mind, there's another name . . . but—I—can't . . . no—

There's a ringing sound in my ears.
The sun catches a little crystal hung on a piece of string on the cur-
tain rod.
Sunlight, refracted through the crystal, splashes little rainbows all over
the kitchen.

There's a moment . . .
and . . .
I . . .
Ringing . . .
I . . .
Colours . . .
Refraction is . . .
white light . . .
You know this. Focus!
Refraction is . . .
colours . . .

I'm so thirsty . . .
The salt . . .
It's the salt . . .

       breathe . . .

I go to the sink and open the tap. Nothing.
I go to the cupboard
get a mug
open the tap. Nothing.
I take the kettle from the stovetop
go the sink to fill the kettle
open the tap. Nothing.
I go to the window
draw the curtains
go to the sink
open the tap. Nothing.

ALIX
Gran?

GRAN
There's no water, Audrey, honey . . .

ALIX
I'm Alix, Gran.

GRAN
No water at all—

ALIX
I know, Gran. I know.

GRAN
How—

ALIX
There hasn't been water in a long time, Gran.

GRAN
Oh. Okay, then.

Eleven

ALIX. EVAN. PORTIA.
Not together.

ALIX
The soldiers have always been here.
Ever since I can remember.

EVAN
The city used to be bigger.
Gran said it was beautiful.
She said if you were to look down into the valley from the hills
you could see everything twinkle.

PORTIA
I open my eyes.
      can't remember what—
      where—

The pool.

ALIX
The military base sits on concrete pillars made to withstand a tidal
surge of four metres.

On the shoreline,
army engineers built a floodgate and a seawall to protect the base and
the town.
Lower-ranking engineering cadets, like Jackson, lift up the structures
every spring.

A road leads from the base into town,
and the road out of town
is always patrolled.

The military base is open to the community:
basic medical facilities
showers, open to the public three nights a week
charging stations
a distribution centre
and of course
the Salt-No machine.

EVAN
When we were kids, our dad brought us out on the water with him,
and at night we'd lay on the deck and look up at the stars.
You can see so many stars out on the water.
It's because there are barely any lights in the hills anymore, he said.
Our dad knows all the stars, all the constellations.
Alix would always fall asleep when he pointed them out but I could
listen for hours.

PORTIA
I'm at the bottom of the pool.
It's early morning.

              thirsty, I'm
              skin is covered in insect bites
              ears ringing

And
              pain

A dull ache in my shoulders
right wrist
swollen from forearm to fingers
              try to move fingers
pain shoots through my arm
head spinning
sweat pours down my forehead.
              relax
              breathe
              broken, this is—
              broken

The sweat burns my eyes.
I wipe it with my left hand
and it comes back covered in blood.
My fingers find a deep cut at the root of my hair.

I press it
nausea
ears ringing louder.

ALIX
Jackson is different.
You can see that he cares.

His father didn't want him joining the army.
His father has money.
Enough money to pay the fine that would allow his son to avoid military service.
The army was not good enough for his only child.
But Jackson told me he wanted to help.
He told me his mom would have been proud.

PORTIA
> breathe
> just breathe
> my heart in my chest

hunched over
propped on my left elbow
I look down

my leg bent at a strange angle
> nausea—
> my leg—
> stop looking at it—

Blackout.

EVAN
One time
I asked my dad what was the point of having a boat if we just stayed here, in the bay.
Couldn't we just take the boat, sail up the shoreline, and leave?

I didn't know about passes and travel bans back then.
Didn't know about the fortified northern cities
and their fleets of patrol boats off their coasts

with orders to shoot first
ask questions never.

We're stuck here.

PORTIA
Wake up again.
Waves of pain and panic coursing through my veins.
    Focus.

One: you fell.
Two: you fell in a pool.
Three: you're hurt.

      breathe
      ears ringing

The bottom of the pool is covered in rotted leaves and debris.
In a corner, a metal porch swing is lying on its side.
Puddles of water everywhere.

Four: there was a storm.
Five: you need help or you're going to die here.

ALIX
Yesterday, in his room
lying on his bed in the dark
Jackson told me he loved me.
Then he said he was sorry.
I asked: sorry for what?
He didn't answer.
I asked again: sorry for what?
He just said: "I wish you hadn't been born here."

Where are you going after?
I asked.
Where are you going after this town is evacuated?
Can I come with you?

He didn't answer.

Twelve

GRAN, frantic. EVAN comes in as she talks. She doesn't recognize him.

GRAN

Listen to me closely. You have to leave right now. You're not safe here, not safe at all. Take this, memorize it: it's an address you'll need to remember. You'll be meeting a man there, and he'll help you when you arrive. Remember this address, remember it. Burn the paper. Don't carry it around with you. Don't enter it anywhere, just find your way there on your own. You have it? 8489 Halston Street, it's a restaurant, you'll get in through a back door in an alley. Repeat it: 8489 Halston Street. Back door. 8489. Burn the paper. Don't just rip it. Burn it.

EVAN

Gran ... ?

GRAN

You come in through the back door. There'll be a man waiting for you. I can't tell you his name. I can't tell you my name. He's tall and has a beard. You can trust him. Grab that grey sweater in the closet, you can take it with you. You can't go back home to get your things. They'll be looking for you. They're probably already looking for you. This needs to happen quickly.

EVAN

Gran ... What's going on?

GRAN
Come to the bathroom. I have to cut your hair. We need you to look different. It'll make you look a little older too, that'll work . . .

EVAN *(taking GRAN's hands in his)*
Gran, it's me, it's Evan.

GRAN
You'll be okay. You'll be fine. I've done this before, get people out of places. I have my ways, my people . . . *(very calm)* You need to calm down. You're leaving in less than an hour, and we need to cut your hair—

EVAN
Gran, do you want to lie down? Do you want to rest for a bit?

> *Beat. Shift.*

GRAN
We need to pack.

EVAN
Yeah, Gran. We need to pack.

GRAN
I— I'm just—

EVAN
It's okay, Gran. Do you want to lie down?

GRAN
She was here. I remember her—she came here.

EVAN
Who was here, Gran?

GRAN
Her name is— Now she's someone else. She—she lived out there. Close to the water. I remember.

EVAN
Do you want me to get Alix, Gran? Do you want me to see if I can find Alix?—

GRAN *(angry)*
I remember. I remember her. I'm not insane, Karl. I'm doing just fine. I don't want to lie down. I remember her. Don't you? She was here. She came here. To this house.

EVAN
Gran . . . ?

Beat. Shift.

GRAN *(softly)*
I want a glass of water.

EVAN
Okay. Why don't you go lie down in your room and I'll bring you a glass of water, okay?

GRAN
You're a good one, Evan. You are.

EVAN
You're a good one too, Gran.

Thirteen

PORTIA

I'm swimming in a pool.
I let all the air out of my nose.
Bubbles rise to the surface.
I curl into a ball.
Sink to the bottom of the pool.
I can hear my own heart beating in my ears.

 ...boom-boom boom-boom...

I'm at the bottom.
It feels cool down here.
No one can see me.
I hear my name.
Coming from very far away.

 ...boom-boom boom-boom...

I open my eyes.
The chlorine burns my eyes.
Above me, I can see the sunshine.
Turquoise beams of light.
I let out another stream of bubbles.
My chest hurts.
My lungs empty.

My body feels heavier and heavier,
sinking all the way down.

A searing pain in my throat.
I take my hands to feel my neck
raw skin opening into gills.
I breathe in water.

The light leaves the pool,
turquoise turning to grey,
my eyes can see in the dark.

It's not a pool anymore.
It was never a pool.

I swim out to sea.
The moonlight and starlight shimmering above.
I disappear into the water.
Sink under the waves.
I am small
minuscule
and the ocean is vast.
I'm going home.

Fourteen

ALIX

I walk over to the base to see Jackson.
The screens are still playing the evacuation order on a loop with a
countdown clock:
twenty-two hours nineteen minutes.

From the community area
I slip out to a hangar where trucks are parked in neat rows
and, from there, to a small door on the far side.
That door is usually never guarded
but now I see two soldiers
talking to each other in hushed voices
hands resting on their guns at their sides.
I hide behind one of the trucks.
A few minutes pass and another soldier joins them.
They talk—I can't hear anything—and suddenly,
the three soldiers exit the hangar by the main doors at the front.
I quickly get to the little door and walk through it.

I walk with my head down to Jackson's door and get in without making
a noise.
He's still sleeping—
he must've been on the night shift.
I slide under the covers with him.

Jackson wakes up, turns on the light, and sits up in his bed.
"How did you get in? The base is on lockdown."
Through the hangar, as usual, I tell him.
Aren't you happy to see me?
He laughs and takes me in his arms.

What's going on, I ask him. Why is the base on lockdown?
"That government lady is missing," he says. "We have her on the
security cameras exiting the east gate yesterday before the storm, then
nothing. Some higher-ups think she may have been kidnapped."
Kidnapped.
Crazy.

We kiss and Jackson weaves his fingers through my hair.
He takes a deep breath.
"I have to tell you something," he says. "Something bad."

Jackson talks, his voice low, his words fast, panicked.
My mind reeling
my throat dry
my fingernails digging into my palms
I can't hear anything after the words
      buses
      floodgates
      water

I'm completely numb
cold dread spreading through my veins.

This was never meant to be a peaceful evacuation.

Four hundred and twenty-nine people live here.
Plus one hundred twenty-three soldiers.
That's five hundred and fifty-two people.
That's ten fifty-six-seat buses.
Maybe a little less for the soldiers riding in military vehicles.
Let's say eight buses.
We should be getting eight buses.

Jackson says the orders came in earlier during the afternoon.

The order for two buses.
Two. Buses.

They'll be able to say they tried.
They really tried to save us.
They just couldn't win against the water.

Jackson cries.
He says he's sorry.
He says he had orders.
They all did.

A few hours ago, the soldiers opened the floodgates.
They calculated that twenty-four hours later,
at three in the morning,
six hours before the deadline they gave us,
the water will reach catastrophic levels on the barrier.

At 3 a.m., alarms will sound.
People will come out of their houses to streets already flooding with
cold water.
To buildings already toppling under the force of the current.
To dangerous debris all around them.

They'll run up to the base with only the clothes on their back. Once the buses and the military vehicles are full, they'll leave. And all that'll be left is this town drowning.

Fifteen

The pool. Humid, hot, muggy.
PORTIA, in and out of consciousness.
EVAN, standing over her.
PORTIA mumbles.
EVAN hands her a can of Salt-No from his bag.

EVAN
Drink this.

PORTIA looks at the label cautiously, drinks it, winces.

Yeah, Salt-No is bad. When you're not used to it.

PORTIA *(very weak)*
I fell in the pool during the storm. I hit my head—

EVAN
This pool is ours. We found it first. This is our stuff; you can't have it.

PORTIA
I wasn't after your stuff . . .

Beat.

Please get me some help. I think my wrist is sprained—my leg is broken. Is it money you want? I can pay—

EVAN
I don't want money.

PORTIA
Everybody wants money.

EVAN
Money stopped being useful around here a long time ago.

PORTIA
You're being relocated. You'll need money when you get out west. Please. I need you to get help.

Beat.

EVAN
What are you doing all the way out here? This sector is condemned.

PORTIA
I had to see it.

Beat. PORTIA *picks up an animal figurine from the ground. It's filthy, covered in silt. She polishes it with her thumb. It's a giraffe.*

Where did you find this?

EVAN *(taking the toy from her)*
It's mine.

EVAN goes to the filtration trap to find the bag of toys. Because of the storm, some of them have been scattered on the bottom of the pool. The bag is waterlogged. While PORTIA talks, EVAN cleans up, wrings out the bag, puts the animals back in, and hides the bag in the trap again.

PORTIA *(softly)*
I had one just like it . . . They came in packs of three. Cheap plastic. They would melt and change shapes if you left them in the sun. Animals, fruits, dinosaurs, cars . . . They called them "surprise packs" because you wouldn't know what you'd get inside. You couldn't see through the bag. I always hated it when I got those boring fruit pieces, or the cars. The animals were the only ones I wanted. My cousin Simon only collected the dinosaurs. We would trade. Animals for me. Dinosaurs for him. Then trade the ones you had in duplicate or triplicate. Until you had your collection. That giraffe . . . I had four of them at some point . . . Take a look at its eyes . . . Do they line up or are they just a bit off? . . .

Beat. EVAN takes the giraffe out of the bag again, looks at it.

EVAN
One is higher than the other. I hadn't even noticed.

PORTIA
Factory error . . . *(lost in thought)* Where did you find them?

EVAN *(defensive)*
Just everywhere. I don't really look for them—I just seem to find them . . . They're not all plastic. I have some that are glass, porcelain, or clay . . .

Beat.

I just like them, that's all. The animals.

PORTIA
Yeah ... I did too.

    Beat.

EVAN
I have some painkillers. I traded some Plexiglas I salvaged for them. I was keeping them for my grandmother, for her arthritis.

    PORTIA looks up to EVAN, shading her eyes from the sun. Beat.

Take them.

PORTIA
Are you sure?

EVAN
I can always get more. *(mocking)* And, you know, all our medical needs will be taken care of once we're evacuated ...

PORTIA
They will.

    Beat. EVAN hands her a little bottle of four pills. She takes it
    with the Salt-No, closes her eyes.

I know how hard it can be to get medication here. Thank you.

EVAN
What are you really doing out here?

PORTIA (*pointing above the lip of the pool*)
There used to be a park over there. Not a beautiful park. There wasn't any grass. Just cracked concrete slabs and dead shrubs covered in dust. My cousin Simon had a rusted bicycle and we used to ride it around the park. He was the only kid here who had a bike until it was stolen by some older kids. They almost killed Simon, beating him with old pipes, splitting his forehead open with broken glass bottles. I remember yelling at him: Give them your bike! Just give it to them! And Simon cried, blood all over his face, but he gave them his bike.

Beat.

This place was called the Mercury Tower. Low-rent units for single mothers.

EVAN
How can you be from this place? That's not possible. You're the government representative.

PORTIA (*lost in thought*)
When you grow up in a place like this, you can't have everything you want.

Beat.

Something happened and I had to leave. There was no other choice. I became someone else. Someone without my past, without my childhood, the childhood I spent here. I never thought I would come here again, but then, this . . . And I had to come.

Beat.

I'm Portia now. Portia Lowell-James. What's your name?

EVAN *(ignoring the question)*
There are travel bans. There have been travel bans for years, you can't just leave.

PORTIA
You can. If you know the right people. I can be that person for you. For your family.

    Beat.

Just get me some help and I'll make sure you and your family are taken care of after the evacuation. Your grandmother with her arthritis taken care of. Help me and I'll help you.

    ALIX gets into the pool. She looks over to PORTIA, confused.

ALIX
Evan? What's going on?

PORTIA *(now knowing EVAN's name)*
Evan . . . Please help me, Evan.

ALIX *(to PORTIA)*
The base is on lockdown. Everyone is looking for you.

PORTIA
Yes, go to the base, please. Tell them where I am and they'll know what to do.

ALIX *(to EVAN)*
I need to talk to you.

EVAN
What is it?

ALIX *(taking EVAN aside)*
They're not telling the truth. About the evacuation.

Beat.

They're lying, the government, the soldiers. They have orders from her and they've been lying to everyone. You can't trust anything she says.

EVAN
What are you talking about?

ALIX comes back to PORTIA with EVAN.

ALIX *(to PORTIA)*
Tell him. Tell him about the orders. You lied to everyone. You stood in front of that camera and lied to this entire town, pretended to care, pretended you were on our side, pretended to have a plan for us . . . But you have nothing. There's no plan. And you keep lying to us, to me, to my brother.

Beat. PORTIA doesn't answer.

EVAN *(looking at ALIX)*
What's going on?

ALIX
We're not being evacuated tomorrow morning, like she said on the broadcast. The soldiers already opened the floodgates and at 3 a.m., six hours before the deadline they gave us, it'll be too late. They're not evacuating us calmly and peacefully. They're drowning this place and

leaving us to fight our way out. There aren't enough buses coming. They're only bringing enough to save face. To pretend like they did something to help us.

She looks over to PORTIA.

It's true, isn't it? This is going to happen?

Back to EVAN.

No one knows about it. No one will be ready. A lot of people are going to die.

Long beat.

PORTIA *(softly)*
It's not what you think . . .

Beat.

(to EVAN*)* I have orders.

ALIX
You can't evacuate an entire town—this entire town—with two buses—

EVAN *(under, to himself)*
Two buses?

ALIX
. . . There are children here. Older people. We need more time. We need eight buses. Nine, even. You have orders? Orders to let everyone who doesn't get to the base on time, in the middle of the night, drown?

PORTIA (*to ALIX*)
Who told you this? Did a soldier at the base tell you this?

ALIX looks away. Beat.

I see . . . He's tall and handsome. And has a sad story about how his mother—or is it his father?—died. Malaria? Lyme disease? Hurricane? He wants to change the world. He just wishes things were different—

ALIX
Shut up.

EVAN
Alix . . .

PORTIA
He says he wants to take you away from this place. I've been where you are now, trust me. He's lying . . . they all lie, these soldiers. Is it the way he looks at you? The way he kisses you? The way he slides his hand down your pants—

ALIX
Shut up!

PORTIA (*very calm*)
Alix. Trust me on this. I know these soldiers. He doesn't care about you, doesn't care about this shithole. He'll forget all about you when his tour ends and it gets him a prime spot in a university or a nice cushy job. He can't help you, or your family. He can't do anything about this.

Beat.

But if you help me now, Alix, I can make all of this better.

Long beat.

EVAN *(to PORTIA)*
Is it true? Have the floodgates already been opened?

PORTIA
Yes.

EVAN
And the alarms will sound at 3 a.m.?

PORTIA
It's what we've calculated.

EVAN
Are there only two buses coming to evacuate this town?

PORTIA
Yes.

EVAN
How can we be on these buses?

ALIX
Evan, you can't be serious . . .

PORTIA *(to EVAN)*
My leg is broken, my wrist could be broken too. I probably have a concussion . . . Get me help and I'll make sure you're on one of those buses.

ALIX
We have to let everyone know. We have to make sure everyone is ready.
If we gather enough people we can march right up to the base commander, tell him we know everything, and demand more time, more
buses. Demand the orders be reversed, demand a real evacuation, in
exchange for her—

PORTIA
This is extortion and this government doesn't negotiate with terrorists.
I'm not important enough for them to make an exception. There are
two buses coming and that's final. You can't win this. Don't die here.

EVAN
She's probably right, Al. We can't win this . . .

> *Beat.*

ALIX *(to EVAN)*
I can't believe you. You can't just accept that some people deserve
to die.

> *Beat. EVAN doesn't answer.*

I can't listen to this—

> *ALIX leaves the pool. EVAN tries to stop her, unsuccessfully. EVAN*
> *looks at PORTIA.*

PORTIA
Listen to me, Evan. Many years ago, someone helped me out of this
place when I needed it. I can do the same for you. If you trust me.

EVAN
I don't trust you.

PORTIA
Do you really have any other choice?

Beat.

Sixteen

THE VOICE OF GRAN, in a time and space of its own.
The audio recording of the evacuation orders.
Loops, effects.
Nightmarish soundscape.
GRAN, alone, opens can after can of Salt-No and pours them on
the ground.

THE VOICE OF GRAN

.... The Anthropocene geological era is the unofficial name that
was given, in the early twenty-first century, to the later part of the
Holocene era . . .

THE VOICE OF PORTIA

. . . The 2067-9K Act . . .

THE VOICE OF GRAN

. . . The Anthropocene refers to an era where we start seeing significant
human impact on the Earth's geology, ecosystems, and climate . . .

THE VOICE OF PORTIA

. . . we do not have enough energy to keep the levees from breaking
under the force of the water . . .

THE VOICE OF GRAN
... Human impact on the planet's geology, ecology, and climatology can be traced back to the eighteenth century's Industrial Revolution ...

THE VOICE OF PORTIA
... living in dangerous times. Let us help you ...

THE VOICE OF GRAN
... One of the symptoms of human impact can be measured in the drastic increase of carbon dioxide in the atmosphere, in the presence of what are called "forever chemicals" in rainwater all over the world, making it unsafe for human consumption ...

> **GRAN** *(to herself)*
> Symptoms.

THE VOICE OF PORTIA
... a total and complete evacuation of this city ...

THE VOICE OF GRAN
... Human impact can also be seen in changes to drainage and water retention patterns all over the world. Road building, dams, canals, deforestation, land-levelling, trenching, desertification ...

THE VOICE OF PORTIA
... property or properties considered under water ...

> **GRAN** *(to herself)*
> Water.

THE VOICE OF PORTIA
... has your best interest at heart. This government cares ...

THE VOICE OF GRAN
... All over the world, human impact can be found embedded in rock ...

> **GRAN** *(to herself)*
> Human impact.

THE VOICE OF GRAN
... traces of chlorine ...

> **GRAN** *(to herself)*
> I'm swimming in a pool.

THE VOICE OF GRAN
... mercury ...

> **GRAN** *(to herself)*
> Mercury.

THE VOICE OF GRAN
... artificial radionuclides ...

> **GRAN** *(to herself)*
> Radionuclides.

THE VOICE OF GRAN
... inorganic ash ...

> **GRAN** *(to herself)*
> Ash.

THE VOICE OF GRAN
... plastic ...

THE VOICE OF PORTIA
Brighter days are ahead.

> *GRAN takes a can of Salt-No, opens it, drinks it.*
> *Water pours down her front.*
> *She drinks.*

Seventeen

EVAN, in the pool. PORTIA.

PORTIA
She's not coming back.

EVAN
She will. She just needs to cool down.

Beat.

PORTIA
We can't keep you here by the shoreline. We're bleeding money keeping this city safe, keeping whatever intermittent power you have running, keeping the army deployed, keeping the seawalls from crumbling. The truth is: we have nothing for you. We have nothing to give, nothing to spare. That's why you're only getting two buses. That's why we're not evacuating everyone. We can't. There's no way. We are just surviving too.

Interior cities are not all shiny, gleaming, golden metropolises. You see it all around you: crimes stats are rising, employment is harder and harder to come by, poverty is everywhere. We like to tell ourselves it's not as bad as here, but as the shorelines become more and more humid and hot, interior cities are becoming drier, hotter. The demand on the grid is always higher, water restrictions are becoming more and more severe, crops in the interior farmlands are failing. The greenhouses are vandalized or taken over by criminal organizations.

It didn't used to be like this. It got like this slowly, over time. And we got used to it. We are adaptable.

Beat.

EVAN
Why even pretend you're evacuating us?

PORTIA
People need to think the government still has the situation under control. People need to think we know what we're doing. When the two buses bring your people to the refugee compounds, no one will ask questions. They won't ask why so few of you. They'll be relieved there's so few of you. We'll tell them about the incident here, the flood, and they'll chalk it up to a mechanical error . . . floodgates fail all the time. People will mourn and say it's a shame, but they'll forget. And that's the way it has to be.

EVAN
Why did you come back here? You knew what was going to happen to us, you knew this evacuation was all a lie, why risk it? You could have just stayed in your city, pushed a button, forgotten about it.

PORTIA
This is home.

Beat.

This was home. At some point . . . It's like something was pulling me back. Currents pulling me back. I needed to see it one last time.

EVAN
Before you destroyed it . . .

Beat. PORTIA holds his gaze.

I want safe conducts: my sister, my grandmother, my—

Small beat.

And me. Three safe conducts. And three city ID cards; not refugee cards, real city IDs: new names, new everything. When we get off that bus in the city, I want us to be able to disappear.

PORTIA
Deal.

Beat.

I'm sorry. If I could save everyone, I would—

EVAN
Don't . . .

Beat.

PORTIA
You're a good person, Evan. You're doing the best you can. We're all doing the best we can.

Beat.

EVAN
Three city ID cards. Nothing less.

PORTIA
Nothing less.

He leaves. PORTIA *stays alone.*

Eighteen

ALIX

I walk back to town through the hole in the barricade.
The road is deserted and the wind carries debris and littles branches on
the cracked asphalt.
The air feels electric and storm clouds are gathering in the distance,
over the water.

I keep to the sides of the road in case I cross paths with a patrol.
They must be out looking for the government representative and it's
always suspicious to be this close to the barricade.

I head home.
I don't know where else to go.

Gran's street probably used to be very beautiful.
Dotted with little white houses and big leafy trees.
But now all the trees are gone,
either from insect invasions brought on by the heat
or from being cut down for firewood to keep the winter damp at bay
when the power was out for weeks at a time.

I see her walking in the distance.
Silhouetted against the grey of the sky.

(shouting) Gran? Gran!

GRAN
Yes?

ALIX
Gran, it's me: Alix.

GRAN (*confused*)
Oh yes . . . Alix . . .

ALIX (*very slowly*)
Your granddaughter. Karl's daughter.

Beat. Shift.

GRAN
I have to go pick up my son Karl at the park. It's almost dark and it looks like there's a storm coming. He hasn't even finished packing his bag and we're leaving tomorrow. He's not happy about us leaving.

ALIX
Leaving to go where, Gran?

GRAN
I'm going on assignment. We'll be away for a year.

ALIX
Okay, Gran, let's get you home.

GRAN (*very confused*)
But . . . Karl . . .

ALIX
I'll pick up Karl and bring him home, okay?

GRAN
That's so nice of you. So nice—

ALIX
Let's get you home.

GRAN
What's your name, again? Did you just move here? Not a lot of people move out here anymore. It's too bad we're leaving tomorrow for my assignment. Do you have kids? No . . . You probably don't . . . You're so young. Karl is ten years old. Not a lot of kids around here anymore . . .

ALIX
Come with me, Gran.

    Beat. Shift.

GRAN
Alix? What are you doing outside in the rain?

ALIX
Why are you outside, Gran?

GRAN
I . . . I— I don't remember anymore . . .

ALIX
It's okay . . . Let's just get you home.

GRAN
I'm sorry. It didn't used to be like this . . .

ALIX
I remember.

GRAN
We're being evacuated tomorrow.

ALIX
Yeah . . . tomorrow . . .

Beat.

They're not evacuating the whole town, Gran. It's all a big lie. I have to do something. Tell me what I should do, Gran. Please.

Beat. Shift.

GRAN
Don't worry about me. I have my Associated Press safe conducts. Everything is very organized. Nothing bad can happen to me or my boy. You take care now. I hope you're still around the neighbourhood when we come back from my assignment.

ALIX
Me too.

Beat.

I walk Gran back to the house.
She's already forgotten all about picking up her son from the park.
She walks into the kitchen, muttering in Latin under her breath.
She stands by the window.

The rain is getting stronger and the wind whistles in the crevices of the old roof.
Gran presses her hand to the window and rests her forehead against the glass.

I grab an old olive-green raincoat from the hook by the door.
I put it on.
It smells like my dad.

I imagine him walking through the door.
He would throw his muddy boots in the bathtub,
sit at the table,
run his hand through his hair,
show us the little treasures he found.

I'd tell him everything.
I'd tell him about the evacuation, and the soldiers opening the flood-gates, and the two buses, and Gran making a scene at the base, and the government representative lying injured at the bottom of our pool, and Evan and I fighting, and I'd tell him about Jackson, and he wouldn't even be mad.
He would talk in a calm voice.
Ask questions.
Be a dad.
He'd know exactly what to do.

    Beat.

I grab a rusted chain and padlock hanging on a nail by the door frame.
I close the door behind me, loop the chain between the door handle and the porch railing.

I lock Gran inside so I can keep her safe.

There's a clap of thunder and rain falls in sheets, turning the cracked street to mud.

I have to find Evan. I can't do this alone.

I pull up the coat's hood over my head and head out in the direction of the pool.

Nineteen

THE VOICE OF GRAN is a memory.

PORTIA

I remember being seventeen and watching a motorcade drive through the old downtown.

My cousin Simon and I sitting on an old rotten fence, watching the black cars glide by.

I don't remember what the politicians were doing here
don't even remember who they were
it doesn't really matter anymore.

"We could kidnap them," Simon said to me. "Kidnap them and ask the government for loads and loads of money for their safe return."

He spoke too loudly. We laughed too loudly.
It just seemed . . . incredibly funny at the time.
People in front started looking back towards us sitting on the fence.
Soldiers started looking at us.
We didn't notice.
A woman grabbed me by the hand and yanked me down to the ground whispering in my ear to shut up.

A soldier walked up to the fence, pushing Simon off, yelling, screaming.
Simon tried to hit the soldier back, but the others surrounded him.

The woman hid me in the crowd that was forming around Simon and the soldier.

She held me back from trying to help my cousin.

THE VOICE OF GRAN

Don't make a sound. Anything you do is going to make things worse for him. I'm a journalist. I've seen things like this happen all over this country.

PORTIA

I looked at the soldiers shoving and kicking Simon.

They ripped out his ID papers from his jacket and pocketed them.

They spat on the ground near his head.

I didn't cry, didn't scream—I just stayed hidden behind the journalist until it was over.

Frozen in place.

Shock.

I watched everyone gathered around not saying a word, pretending it wasn't happening.

I wanted to kill all of them.

I wanted to scream.

But I couldn't move.

It only lasted a minute or two.

We could still see the motorcade out in the distance.

Simon wasn't moving, but he was still breathing, his belly rising and falling.

THE VOICE OF GRAN

They took his papers. They'll know who he is. And they'll find you, your family, soon enough. You have to go. Now. Follow me.

PORTIA
I did. I followed her.
I trusted her. I don't know why.
I left Simon on the ground, slowly rising to his feet, holding on to the fence.
I. Left. Him. There.
No one dared to help him, even with the soldiers going back to their post alongside the road.

I followed the journalist to a little white house shaded by an old rotten tree.
Sitting on a low branch, a little boy, six or seven years old, stares out at me.
This was a nice part of town.
I had never been there before.

It was all a blur . . .

Photos and papers and passport and safe conducts and a birth certificate with a name that wasn't mine and a sweater that smelled like mildew and sitting on a bus after shoving my fake passport in a soldier's face.

The bus slowly making its way west.
Controls.
Checkpoints.
Every time I took the fake documents out of my bag, I thought:

It won't work.

But I was waved through every time.
Days later, I got to the city, went to the place the journalist told me to go,
and a tall slender man gave me registration papers with my new name and a school ID card.
"Students IDs are easier to forge," he said.

"And you're young enough for it to work."

I can't pay for school. There's no way I can pay for school, I told him.

"It's all taken care of," he said. "She did you a solid."

I tried looking for her the first few years
tried looking for Simon, tried to know what happened after I left.
I always searched from public computers—just in case—
but I didn't know the journalist's name
didn't know who she worked for.
I walked around the city hoping to see her
there were these compounds where journalists stayed when they came
to the city.

Time passed and I forgot my old name. Forgot this place. My mother.
Simon.
Forgot everything.
After school, I was recruited by an agency to do paperwork for a gov-
ernment office.

Once, from an encrypted computer at work, I looked up Simon's name.
And there, on the screen, I saw his name appear.
His last known address at the Mercury Tower Apartments
and then at the bottom of the screen, the words:

THE VOICE OF GRAN
"Insurgent. Killed."

PORTIA
And a date, just a few days after my escape.
I typed in my mother's name.
Her face jumped out at me.

Older. Sadder. Thin.
Under her picture the words:

THE VOICE OF GRAN
"Deceased. No relations."

PORTIA
Less than a year after I left.
She died not knowing where I was.
Not knowing anything.

I typed in my name
my real name
and under an old picture of me—
I looked so young—
there was only one word:

THE VOICE OF GRAN
"Deceased."

PORTIA
I'm a ghost.

Twenty

EVAN

I head towards the base.

The rain is falling so hard you can barely see.

ALIX

Walking downhill towards the pool.

The hood of the green raincoat is covering half of my face.

My shoes are soaked through.

Walk, just keep walking.

EVAN

Get to the base.

Find the community liaison officer.

Have him bring me to the field office.

Tell them I know where the government official is.

Tell them I found her by accident.

Tell them she's injured and needs help.

They'll take care of her and she'll sign the safe conducts.

The sky is dark.

Thunder rumbles in the distance.

ALIX
She did this.
I'll get to the pool, look her in the eyes, and then—
Then I'll—
I don't even know what I'm going to do.
Find Evan.
I need to find Evan.
I stand in the rain.
I can't move.
I breathe in.
Out.
My heart beats in my ears.
Water droplets roll down my nose.

EVAN & ALIX
And then I hear it.

    Sirens.

EVAN
When the water reaches a certain level on the barrier: alarms sound.

ALIX
It's too early.
Way too early.
It's not even eight o'clock.
It just feels darker because of the rain.

EVAN
It's too early. It has to be a mistake.

ALIX

I try to see through the rain.
Everything is dark.
The hood of the green coat keeps falling over my eyes.

EVAN

Through the rain, I see headlights in the distance.
A military vehicle.

EVAN waves down the military vehicle.

ALIX

Towards the shoreline: the pool.
Up the road: the base.
The two buses.
It's too early. The two buses won't be arriving for hours.
Alarms blare.
I can't breathe.

EVAN

I jump into the mud on the side of the road as the military vehicle
speeds past me
and then stops a few metres over.
What's going on? I yell over the sound of the alarms.

A soldier, one hand on his gun, one hand on the wheel, wearing half
his uniform:
"Get out of here, man! They didn't take the storm into account. Didn't
take into account the open gates wouldn't be able to contain the added
pressure of the rainwater. They didn't plan it right. We need to get out
of here before the road washes away. There's no time, man. No time."

ALIX

My mind flashes back to the metal chain holding the door shut at home.

EVAN

Take me with you! I scream. We can find my sister, my grandmother. Please!

"I can't do anything. We're full up in here."

In the darkness of the back seat, four sets of eyes look out at me.
Each one of them looking scared.
Each one of them not much older than me.
Squeezed in the corner, I see Jackson.

ALIX

This is my fault.
I should have gone to the base right away,
told them I knew where the government official was.
Told them I knew everything: the floodgates, the buses.
Told them we needed more time, we needed help, we needed more.

EVAN

Jackson! I'm Alix's brother. I'm her brother. Please, we have to find her.

He looks down.
He turns away from me, as much as he can in the cramped back seat.

You're supposed to help us!
I'm yelling at them.

I reach for the truck's door.
The soldier lifts his gun.
Points it at me.

EVAN, arms above his head, slowly backs away.

The truck starts up again and drives off into the distance.

ALIX
I run towards home
my shoes slipping in the rivers of mud.
I have to get home.
Home.
Gran.

EVAN
I stand in the rain.
Another truck rushes past me, full of soldiers.
Three of them are even standing on the footholds,
their muscles straining to hold on to the roof, slick with rain.
I have to find Alix. Gran.

Slowly, the light rises on GRAN.

I think of the bag of little toys in the pool's filtration trap.

THE VOICE OF GRAN / GRAN
Polar bear?

EVAN
Ursus maritimus.

THE VOICE OF GRAN / GRAN
Tiger?

EVAN
Panthera tigris tigris.

THE VOICE OF GRAN / GRAN
Dolphin?

EVAN
Tursiops truncatus.

THE VOICE OF GRAN / GRAN
Chimpanzee?

EVAN
Pan troglodytes.

THE VOICE OF GRAN / GRAN
White shark?

EVAN
Carcharodon carcharias.

And the little giraffe with its crooked eyes:

THE VOICE OF GRAN / GRAN & EVAN
Giraffa camelopardalis.

EVAN
She thought I didn't listen.
But I remember all of their names.
Their Latin names.
The only ones that matter, she told me once.

I run through yards.
I push my way through panicked people heading towards the base.
They're dropping their bags to run faster,

scattered clothes shining pale in the rainy darkness.
I'm almost there.

ALIX
The wind pushes the coat's hood away from my head.
The water in my hair drops down my neck.
It's cold and warm at the same time.
My mind flashes to Jackson for a moment.
Just a moment.

EVAN & ALIX
I get to a large ditch near Gran's street.

ALIX
The water, usually just a trickle at the bottom, is now a raging river.
Waist high. Maybe more.

EVAN
The air smells like rot and salt.

ALIX
Pieces of driftwood rush past.
Debris, pieces of plastic.

EVAN
The water in the ditch keeps rising.

ALIX & EVAN
There's no way around it.

ALIX
Not without losing so much time.

ALIX & EVAN
Alarms are not as loud here.

EVAN
Or maybe it's just because of the sound of the water.

ALIX & EVAN
I look at the water.
It can't be that deep . . .

ALIX
There's someone else standing by the ditch.
Further downstream.
Even in the rain and dark, I recognize him.
(screams) Evan!

EVAN
I hear my name.
I recognize the voice without seeing her.
I run to her, my feet slipping in the mud,
falling face down
getting up again.
Alix.

ALIX and EVAN stand at the edge of the river.

They left. The soldiers.

ALIX
We need to get to Gran. She's home. She's alone. We can't leave her alone.

Beat. They look at the water.

EVAN
We can wade across the ditch. Hold on to me.

They hold hands.
Inhale deeply.

Epilogue

The sound of water.
Darkness.
ALIX. EVAN. GRAN. PORTIA. Silhouettes.

PORTIA
... Four little plastic giraffes all lined up on the shelf above my bed ...
... three of them had crooked eyes ...
... out my bedroom window on the seventh floor ...
... I could see ...
... a pool ...
... shining turquoise in the sunlight ...

ALIX & EVAN
I'm swimming in a pool.

ALIX
The water is cool and clear and the sun makes the surface of the water shimmer.
My body glides gently on the surface
breaking through the water
without a sound.

PORTIA
I used to be so good at holding my breath underwater.

ALIX & EVAN
I'm swimming in a pool.

EVAN
All around me the trees are green and a gentle breeze makes the high
branches sway.

PORTIA
Currents brought me back.

ALIX
I get to the middle of the pool and roll over onto my back
my body caressed by the sunshine
my breath calm and slow.

EVAN
The sky is very blue.

ALIX & EVAN
A voice
my gran's voice
whispers in my ear:

GRAN
It used to be like this.
It used to be exactly like this.

PORTIA
Cities sink from the bottom up.
Now you know.

ALIX
It's like my body forgets how to swim
how to stay above the water.

EVAN
I'm thrashing in the turquoise waters of the pool
my head bobs in and out of the water
I swallow large gulps of water
it tastes like salt.

PORTIA
Listen to the sound of your heartbeat.
boom-boom boom-boom

ALIX
I slowly sink to the bottom
my eyes open and burning
my lungs spasming in my chest.

GRAN
Drowning is actually like being poisoned from the inside.
The urge to breathe comes from the bloodstream becoming saturated
by carbon dioxide.
The lack of oxygenated blood sends a signal to the brain to

ALIX, EVAN, GRAN, & PORTIA
inhale

ALIX
Water fills my body.
Life leaks out.
All around me the pool water becomes murkier.

EVAN
Sediments fall to the bottom of the pool.

ALIX
Algae blooms in a time-lapse.
Insects are born.

EVAN
Birds and amphibians feed on them.
Animals come to drink, to hide in the trees.

GRAN & EVAN
Procyon lotor.
Ondatra zibethicus.
Lithobates catesbeianus.

EVAN
Birds return.
Building nests high up in the ruins of us.
We are erased.
Millimetre by millimetre.

> *A white floodlight emits a blinding white light.*
> *Only for a moment.*
> *Then darkness returns.*

THE VOICE OF GRAN
An ecosystem is a community of interconnected living and non-living
elements, functioning as an open, or closed ecological unit.

PORTIA
I'm going home

ALIX & EVAN
Life moves back into the pool.
Life breathes in and out
   in and out
     in and out

GRAN
     in and out
Life heals.

 End.

Acknowledgements

Thank you to Sean Devine, Mary Ellis, Brad Long, and Kyle Ahluwalia from Horseshoes & Hand Grenades Theatre, as well as Eric Coates from the Great Canadian Theatre Company and Emma Tibaldo of Playwrights' Workshop Montréal, who supported the writing of this play.

This play was first imagined during a playwriting retreat at the lovely home of Amanda West Lewis and Tim Wynne-Jones in 2016. Thank you to all the beautiful humans who were there during that weekend. I will always cherish these moments (and remember the amazing food!).

Thank you to my agent Catherine Mensour. You are extraordinary in all ways.

Thank you, thank you to director Nicholas Leno, who dove into this play with intelligence, calm, and sensitivity. You created the beautiful and intimate piece I had hoped for when writing it. And your love of coffee that rivals my own made me feel understood.

And lastly, an immense thank you to dramaturg Emily Pearlman, who worked with me on *Shorelines* for almost two years. Your insights, your questions, and your encouragements made this play what it is today.

Mishka Lavigne (she/her) is a playwright, screenwriter, and literary translator based in Ottawa/Gatineau. Her plays have been produced and developed in Canada, Switzerland, France, Germany, Australia, Haiti, Mexico, Romania, and the United States. Her play *Havre* was awarded the 2019 Governor General's Literary Award for Drama (French). Her play *Copeaux*, a movement-based poetic creation piece with director Éric Perron, premiered in Ottawa in March 2020 and was also awarded the Governor General's Literary Award for Drama in 2021 as well as the Prix littéraire Jacques-Poirier. *Albumen*, her first play written in English, received the Prix Rideau Award for Outstanding New Creation in 2019 and the QWF Playwriting Prize in 2020. Mishka is currently working on a bilingual opera libretto with Montreal composer Tim Brady and on four new creations in French, as well as on some translation and screenwriting projects.